¡VAMOS DE FIESTA!

A Harcourt Spanish Reading / Language Arts Program

Fiesta fonémica

CANCIONES Y ACTIVIDADES PARA DESARROLLAR LA CONCIENCIA FONÉMICA

Harcourt

Orlando   Boston   Dallas   Chicago   San Diego

Visite *The Learning Site*
www.harcourtschool.com

For permission to translate/reprint copyrighted material, grateful acknowledgment is made to the following sources:

Maximo Aguirre Music Publishing Company: Music and lyrics from "Todo lo que tengo" (Retitled: "Todo lo que como") by Alberto Lozano de la Vega.

Boy Scouts of America: "One Finger, One Thumb" from *The Boy Scout Songbook*. Music and lyrics copyright © 1970 by Boy Scouts of America.

T.S. Denison & Company, Inc.: "Gum-Ball Machine" from *Action Songs and Rhythms for Children* by Lois Lunt Metz. Music and lyrics copyright © 1962 by T.S. Denison & Co., Inc.

El Colegio de México, AC: Poem #102, 103, 110 and 115 (Retitled: "En la calle del ocho," "Garratilla, zapatilla," "En un plato de ensalada," and "Tin, marín") from *Naranja dulce, limón partido* by Mercedes Díaz Roig and María Teresa Miaja. Text © by El Colegio de México.

Editorial Grijalbo, S.A. de C.V.: Untitled poems (Titled: "A Cuesta le cuesta," "Col, caracol y ajo," "En el trapecio de Trípoli," "Éste le dijo a éste," "Mi hermana Ana," "Mirando, mirando," "Pepe Peña," "Salas sala su salsa," and "Si Panchita plancha") from *El libro de los trabalenguas* by Carmen Bravo-Villasante. Text © by Mondadori España, S.A.; text © 1991 by Editorial Grijalbo, S.A. de C.V.

Editorial Trillas, S.A. de C.V., México: "Caballito blanco" from *Recreo español 1* by María Paz Berruecos, Graciela González de Tapia, and Elisa González Mendoza. Music and lyrics © 1993 by Editorial Trillas, S.A. de C.V.

Dee Gibson: Music and lyrics from "If You Had One Cat" by Dee Gibson in *Songs to Brighten Your Day* by Dee Gibson and Joe Scruggs.

Gobierno del Estado de Campeche y Dirección General de Cultura Popular Secretaría de Educación Pública: "La pelota," "Tu gusto no gusta del gusto," "En la calle 24," and "Toc, toc" from *Los niños de Campeche cantan y juegan.*

Manuel Guerra: Lyrics and music from "Me regalaron un violín" in *Let's Play Games in Spanish* by Loretta Burke Hubp.

Florence Parry Heide: Lyrics by Florence Parry Heide from "Wheels" in *Songs to Sing About Things You Think About*. Lyrics © 1971 by Florence Parry Heide.

Little Simon, an imprint of Simon & Schuster Children's Publishing Division: "Sarasponda" from *The Fireside Book of Fun and Game Songs*, collected and edited by Marie Winn, musical arrangements by Allan Miller. Lyrics and music copyright © 1974 by Marie Winn and Allan Miller.

Lothrop, Lee & Shepard Books, a division of William Morrow & Company, Inc.: Music from "Did You Ever See a Lassie?" in *Singing Bee!* by Jane Hart. Music copyright © 1982 by Jane Hart.

Monte Avila Editores Latinoamericana C.A.: "En la feria…," "Periquito," "¡Oh, Susana!," and "Chófer, Chófer" from *Si canto…soy un cantueso* by Josefina Urdaneta. Lyrics and music © 1995 by Monte Avila Editores Latinoamericana C.A.

NTC/Contemporary Publishing Group: Unititled poems (Titled: "Tres tristes tigres" and "La bailarina") from *Let's Play Games in Spanish* by Loretta Burke Hubp. Text copyright © 1986, 1980 by National Textbook Company.

Oficina Regional de Educación de la UNESCO para América Latina y el Caribe (OREALC): Music and lyrics from "En la despensa" by Judith Acoschky and "Cinco ratoncitos" in *Eduquemos con Música* by Raquel Ojeda Leiva.

Scholastic Inc.: "¡Qué linda manito!" from *Arroz con leche*, selected by Lulu Delacre, musical arrangement by Ana-María Rosado. Lyrics and musical arrangement copyright © 1989 by Lulu Delacre.

Silver Burdett Ginn: "A Ram Sam Sam," Moroccan folk song from *Silver Burdett Music*. Lyrics and music © 1974 by Silver Burdett Ginn.

William Van Clief: Music by Sylvia Worth Van Clief from "Wheels" in *Songs to Sing About Things You Think About*. Music © 1971 by Sylvia Worth Van Clief.

Warner Bros. Publications U.S., Inc., Miami, FL 33014: "El gusanito medidor" by L. Gilda Rincón, M. Valentín Rincón, and A. p. P. Omar Barroso Rincón. Lyrics and music © 1977 by Warner/Chappell Music Mexico, S.A. de C.V.

Every effort has been made to locate the copyright holders for the selections in this work. The publisher would be pleased to receive information that would allow the correction of any omissions in future printings.

Printed in the United States of America

ISBN 0-15-315855-7

07 08 09 10 282 08 07 06 05

CONTENIDO

Canciones/*Songs*

¿Qué es la conciencia fonémica?

La conciencia fonémica es, tal como sugiere el término, reconocer fonemas en el lenguaje hablado. Es entender que el lenguaje se compone de pequeñas unidades, o fonemas, que al unirse forman unidades mayores tales como sílabas, palabras, frases y oraciones. Por ejemplo, la palabra gato se compone de cuatro sonidos individuales: */g/-/a/-/t/-/o/*. Debido a la regularidad de la relación sonido-letra del idioma español, una vez que los niños aprenden los sonidos de las vocales y las consonantes, el proceso de decodificación se concentra en el reconocimiento de fonemas silábicos.

El reconocimiento de fonemas puede resultar difícil para los niños pequeños porque requiere un cambio de atención, del contenido a la forma del lenguaje. Requiere que al hablar, el individuo preste atención al sonido del lenguaje separándolo de su significado.

Los niños que han desarrollado la conciencia fonémica pueden:

- reconocer rimas.
- combinar sonidos para formar palabras.
- identificar cuántos sonidos y sílabas se escuchan en una palabra.
- dividir las palabras habladas en sonidos y sílabas.
- sustituir sonidos y sílabas en palabras habladas.
- añadir sonidos y sílabas a las palabras habladas.
- eliminar sonidos y sílabas a palabras habladas.

En otras palabras, los individuos que dominan la conciencia fonémica pueden contestar correctamente las siguientes preguntas:

What Is Phonemic Awareness?

Phonemic awareness is, as the term suggests, an awareness of phonemes in the speech stream. It is the insight that speech consists of small units—phonemes—that blend together to form larger units of speech such as syllables, words, phrases and sentences. The spoken word gato (cat) is made up of four sounds: */g/-/a/-/t/-/o/*. Due to the regularity of the sound-letter relationship in the Spanish language, once children have learned the vowels and consonants, the emphasis of learning to decode focuses on developing awareness of syllabic phonemes.

Phonemic awareness can be difficult for young children because it demands a shift in attention from the content of speech to the form of speech. It requires individuals to attend to the sounds of speech separate from the meanings.

Children who are phonemically aware are able to do the following:

- rhyme.
- blend isolated sounds together to form a word.
- tell how many sounds and syllables can be heard in a word.
- segment spoken words into sounds and syllables.
- substitute sounds and syllables in spoken words.
- add sounds and syllables to spoken words.
- delete a sound or syllable from a spoken word.

In other words, children who are phonemically aware are able to answer correctly the following questions:

Rima

¿Riman estas palabras?

vamos – ramos (sí)

dame – mesa (no)

correr – jugar (no)

Combinar sonidos y sílabas

¿Qué palabra formamos cuando combinamos estos sonidos?

/s/-/o/-/l/ (sol)

¿Qué palabra formamos cuando combinamos estas sílabas?

/ni/ /do/ (nido)

/lu/ /pa/ (lupa)

/pa/ /lo/ /ma/ (paloma)

Contar sonidos y sílabas

¿Cuántos sonidos escuchas en estas palabras?

pan (1)

¿Cuántas sílabas escuchas en estas palabras?

vaso (2)

pollito (3)

tú (1)

Sonidos y sílabas individuales

¿Qué sonido escuchas al principio de la palabra *rosa*?

(/r/)

¿Qué sílaba escuchas al principio de la palabra *tuya*?

(/tu/)

¿Qué sílaba escuchas al final de la palabra *dedo*?

(/do/)

¿Qué sílaba escuchas en el medio de la palabra *camino*?

(/mi/)

Dividir palabras en sonidos y sílabas

¿Qué sonidos escuchas en esta palabra?

mil (/m/-/i/-/l/)

Rhyme

Do these words rhyme?

vamos (let's go) – ramos (bunches) (yes)

dame (give me) – mesa (table) (no)

correr (run) – jugar (play) (no)

Phoneme and Syllable Blending

What word do we have when we put these sounds together?

/s/-/o/-/l/ (sol) *(sun)*

What words do we have when we put these syllables together?

/ni/-/do/ (nido) *(nest)*

/lu/-/pa/ (lupa) *(magnifying glass)*

/pa/-/lo/-/ma/ (paloma) *(dove)*

Phoneme and Syllable Counting

How many sounds do you hear in this word?

pan (bread) (1)

How many syllables do you hear in these words?

vaso (glass) (2)

pollito (chick) (3)

tú (you) (1)

Phoneme and Syllable Isolation

What is the beginning sound in *rosa* (rose)?

(/r/)

What is the beginning syllable in *tuya* (yours)? (/tu/)

What is the final syllable in *dedo* (finger)?

(/do/)

What is the middle syllable in *camino* (walk)? (/mi/)

Segment Words in Phonemes and Syllables

What sounds do you hear in this word?

mil (one thousand) (/m/-/i/-/l/)

¿Qué sílabas escuchas en estas palabras?

perro (/pe/ /rro/)

lobo (/lo/ /bo/)

conejo (/co/ /ne/ /jo/)

Sustituir sonidos y sílabas

¿Qué palabra formamos si cambiamos /s/ en *sol* por /c/?

(col)

¿Qué palabra formamos si cambiamos la sílaba /lu/ en *luna* por /cu/?

(cuna)

¿Qué palabra formamos si cambiamos la sílaba /me/ en *comemos* por /mi/?

(comimos)

Agregar sílabas

¿Qué palabra formamos si agregamos /pa/ al comienzo de *loma*?

(paloma)

¿Qué palabra formamos si agregamos /pi/ en el medio de *pato*?

(papito)

¿Qué palabra formamos si agregamos /ta/ al final de *pelo*?

(pelota)

Quitar sílabas

¿Qué palabra formamos si quitamos /lle/ del medio de *galleta*?

(gata)

¿Qué palabra formamos si quitamos /re/ del comienzo de *rebaño*?

(baño)

¿Qué palabra formamos si quitamos /te/ del final de *tomate*?

(toma)

What syllables do you hear in these words?

perro (dog) (/pe/-/rro/)

lobo (wolf) (/lo/-/bo/)

conejo (rabbit) (/co/-/ne/-/jo)

Phoneme and Syllable Substitution

What word would we have if we change the /s/ in *sol* (sun) to a /c/?

(col) *(cabbage)*

What word would we have if we change the syllable /lu/ in *luna* (moon) to /cu/?

(cuna) *(cradle)*

What word would we have if we change the syllable /me/ in *comemos* (we eat) to /mi/?

(comimos) *(we ate)*

Syllable Addition

What word would we have if we added /pa/ to the beginning of *loma* (hill)?

(paloma) *(dove)*

What word would we have if we added /pi/ to the middle of *pato* (duck)?

(papito) *(daddy)*

What word would we have if we added /ta/ to the end of *pelo* (hair)?

(pelota) *(ball)*

Syllable Deletion

What word would we have if we left the syllable /lle/ out of the middle of *galleta* (cracker)?

(gata) *(cat)*

What word would we have if we left the syllable /re/ off the beginning of *rebaño* (flock)?

(baño) *(bathroom)*

What word would we have if we left the syllable /te/ off the end of *tomate* (tomato)?

(toma) *(you take)*

Juegos de palabras

Hay una maravillosa tradición oral en la cual los trabalenguas, cantos para equipos y para brincar la soga son pasados de generación en generación y de un niño a otro. Estas actividades son un excelente ejemplo del interés y la fascinación que ejerce, tanto en niños como en adultos, la manipulación del lenguaje. En esta sección encontrará algunos trabalenguas, cantos para equipos y para brincar la soga muy conocidos; también hay sugerencias para otros juegos orales cuyo propósito es la manipulación de sonidos.

Trabalenguas

Los trabalenguas son frases u oraciones difíciles de decir rápidamente, debido a la aliteración o a la secuencia de sonidos similares con estructuras irregulares. Los niños no sólo disfrutan el reto de repetir un trabalenguas, sino también al trabarse con los sonidos, adquieren conciencia de la base fonológica del lenguaje. A continuación encontrará trabalenguas populares que podrá utilizar en parte o en su totalidad. Los trabalenguas cortos (o en ciertos casos, el primer verso de los largos) son apropiados para los niños pequeños. El objetivo es repetirlos una y otra vez, cada vez más rápido. Los niños mayores podrán aprender los trabalenguas más largos y será suficiente reto el poderlos decir completos.

Cantos para equipos

Los cantos para equipos usualmente incluyen rimas de palabras sin sentido y sonidos repetitivos.

Cantos para brincar la soga

Los cantos para brincar la soga, con su ritmo constante, usan muchas veces palabras sin sentido y rimas repetitivas. Muchas de las rimas que ofrecemos a continuación se usan también con juegos de pelota.

Word Play Activities

There is a wonderful oral tradition in which toungue twisters, counting-out chants, and jump-rope rhymes are passed from generation to generation and from one child to another. These verbal activities are excellent examples of children's (and adults') interest in and fascination with manipulating language. Some well-known tongue twisters, counting-out chants, and jump-rope rhymes, along with suggestions for other verbal games that focus on the manipulation of sounds, are provided in this section.

Tongue Twisters

Tongue twisters are phrases or sentences that are difficult to say fast, usually because of an alliteration or a sequence of nearly similar sounds that involves irregular patterns of sounds. Children enjoy the challenge of trying to articulate tongue twisters while at the same time—as they stumble over sounds—their consciousness of the phonological basis of language is being raised. Listed here are some common tongue twisters that may be used in whole or in part. Short tongue twisters (or, in some cases, the first line of longer tongue twisters) are appropriate for younger children; the object is to say them over and over again as quickly as possible. Older children may be able to master the longer tongue twisters, and saying them once all the way through is challenge enough.

Counting-Out Chants

Counting-out chants typically include rhyming nonsense words and patterns of sounds.

Jump-Rope Rhymes

Jump-rope rhymes, with their steady beat, often make use of nonsense words and rhyme patterns. Many of the rhymes we provide here are used also with ball bouncing.

Trabalenguas

A Cuesta le cuesta
subir la cuesta,
y en medio de la cuesta,
va y se acuesta.

Busca el bosque Francisco,
un vasco bizco muy brusco.
Y al verlo, le dijo un chusco:
¿busca el bosque, vasco bizco?

Col, caracol y ajo;
ajo, caracol y col;
col, caracol y ajo;
ajo, caracol y col.

En el trapecio de Trípoli,
trabajan tristemente trastocados
tres tristes trogloditas.

Éste, le dijo a éste,
que fuera donde éste,
para que éste,
mandara a éste,
donde éste;
si éste no va con éste,
menos irá éste con éste.

Mi hermana
Ana,
teje en la ventana
con lana.
Del paso
al piso,
del piso
al paso.

Mirando, mirando,
se corre por el campo,
corriendo por el campo
todos van mirando
que en el campo
se vive corriendo
y mirando.

Pepe Peña
pela papa,
pica piña,
pita un pito,
pica piña,
pela papa,
Pepe Peña.

Salas sala su salsa
con sal de Sales.
Si sales de Sales con sal,
sala la salsa de Sales.

Si Panchita placha
con una planchita,
¿Con cuántas planchas
plancha Panchita?

En un plato tres tristes
tigres toman té y trigo.

Tu gusto no gusta del gusto
que gusta mi gusto.
Si tu gusto gustara
del gusto que gusta mi gusto,
gustaría tu gusto del gusto
que gusta mi gusto.
Hecelchakán

Erre con erre cigarro
erre con erre barril
rápido corren los carros
cargados de azúcar del ferrocarril.

Sólo sé una cosa,
Sólo sé que no sé nada.
Aristóteles

La bailarina baila como una
ballena, porque va llena
de avellanas.

Cantos para equipos

A la víbora de la mar

A la víbora, víbora de la mar,
por aquí pueden pasar.
La de adelante corre mucho.
La de atrás se quedará.
Tras, tras, tras.
Una mexicana que fruta vendía,
ciruela, chabacano,* melón y sandía.
Verbena, verbena, jardín de matatena,
verbena, verbena, jardín de matatena.

albaricoque

En la calle del ocho

En la calle del ocho
me encontré a Pinocho,
y me dijo que contara
del uno al ocho:
1,2,3,4,5,6,7,8.

En un plato de ensalada

En un plato de ensalada
todos comen a la vez.
Churumbel, churumbel,
sota, caballo y rey.

Garratilla, zapatilla

Garratilla, zapatilla,
pies de gato, veinticuatro,
veinticinco, veintiséis,
veintisiete, veintiocho,
veintinueve, treinta.

Tin, marín

Tin, marín,
de do, pingüé,
cúcara, mácara,
títere fue.
Cuantas patas
tiene el gato,
1, 2, 3 y 4.

La pelota

Una mañanita
muy tempranita
me levanté,
me lavé la cara,
me peiné,
bajé al jardín,
me arrodillé,
corté una flor,
se me cayó;
vino mi novio,
me la recogió.
Con una mano,
con la otra,
mueve un pie,
mueve el otro,
molinillo,
palmaditas,
media vuelta,
vuelta entera,
caballito
y juego terminado.

(Calkiní)

Matarile rile rón

Ambos a dos
matarile rile rile
ambos a dos
matarile rile rón

¿Qué quiere usted?
matarile rile rile
¿Qué quiere usted?
matarile rile rón

Yo quiero un paje
matarile rile rile
yo quiero un paje
matarile rile rón

¿Cuál paje se va a llevar?
matarile rile rile
¿Cuál paje se va a llevar?
matarile rile rón

Me llevaré a [fulanito]
matarile rile rile
me llevaré a [fulanito]
matarile rile rón

¿Qué oficio le va a dar?
matarile rile rile
¿Qué oficio le va a dar?
matarile rile rón

Le pondré [oficio]
matarile rile rile
le pondré [oficio]
matarile rile rón

[Ella/El] dice que no le gusta
matarile rile rile
[ella/el] dice que no le gusta
matarile rile rón

Pues le pondremos [otro oficio]
matarile rile rile
pues le pondremos [otro oficio]
matarile rile rón

[Ella/El] dice que sí le gusta
matarile rile rile
[ella/el] dice que sí le gusta
matarile rile rón

Celebremos todos juntos
matarile rile rile
celebremos todos juntos
matarile rile rón

Cantos para brincar la soga

A la una

A la una sale la Luna.
A las dos suena el reloj.
A las tres cojito es.
A las cuatro doy un salto.
A las cinco doy un brinco.
A las seis no me ves.
A las siete anda, vete.
A las ocho ten bizcocho.
A las nueve toma nieve.
Y a las diez, otra vez.

En la calle 24

En la calle 24
una vieja empujó a un gato
con la punta del zapato.
El zapato se rompió
y la vieja se asustó.

Chile, tomate y cebolla,
échale toda la olla.

Ciudad del Carmen

Salta la cuerda

—Salta la cuerda.
—Sáltala tú.
—Salto la cuerda.
—¡Salto la U!

Alma Flor Ada

Toc toc

Toc toc.
—¿Quién va?
El cartero.
—¿Cuántas cartas?
¿Para quién?
—Para Lupe.
Doce.
—Uno dos tres cuatro
cinco seis siete ocho
nueve diez once doce.

Hopelchén

Una, dola

Una, dola,
tela, catola,
quile, quilete,
estaba la reina
en su gabinete.
Vino Gil,
apagó el candil,
candil, candilón.
Cuéntalas bien
que las veinte son.

Estaba una viejita

Estaba una viejita
juntando su leñita.
llegó la lloviznita
y corrió y corrió
para su cuevita.

Uno, dos, tres

Uno, dos, tres,
cuatro, cinco, seis,
siete, ocho,
nueve y diez.
¿Qué quiero ser?
Doctor, abogado,
maestro, juez,
panadero, arquitecto,
enfermera,
[Los niños siguen nombrando carreras
hasta que pierda el jugador que salta.]

Chocolate

Uno, dos, tres: CHO
uno, dos, tres: CO
uno, dos, tres: LA
uno, dos, tres: TE
bate, bate, CHOCOLATE

Formar palabras

Cunningham y Cunningham (1992) describen una actividad llamada *Formar palabras*, en la cual los niños dividen palabras presentadas oralmente en sus fonemas individuales y colocan tarjetas de letras para representar las palabras escritas. Esta actividad aumenta el conocimiento y la comprensión de la relación sonido-letra especialmente en los niños que tienen algún conocimiento de la relación entre letras y sonidos.

En esta actividad, se le entregan a cada niño unas tarjetas con letras previamente seleccionadas. Luego, se les pide que usen las tarjetas para formar palabras, comenzando con palabras de dos letras y aumentando progresivamente hasta que en la última palabra deben usar todas las letras que les entregaron. Por ejemplo, se entrega a los niños tarjetas con las letras *a, o, g, l* y *s*. (Los Cunningham sugieren que los niños coloquen estas tarjetas en el siguiente orden: primero, las vocales y luego, las consonantes en orden alfabético.) Luego la maestra les pide que seleccionen las dos tarjetas que forman la palabra *lo*. Los niños mueven las tarjetas *l* y *o* para formar la palabra. Después, la maestra les pide que cambien una letra para formar la palabra *la*. Luego les sugiere que añadan una letra para formar *las*. También se les puede pedir que formen la palabra *los* y que luego inviertan el orden de las letras para formar *sol*, enfatizando que en las palabras el orden de las letras es importante. De ahí en adelante se les pedirá a los niños que formen las palabras *sola, algo, lago, lagos* y finalmente la palabra *salgo*.

Manipular las tarjetas de letras para escribir palabras exige que los niños centren su atención en el sonido de las palabras. La maestra puede continuar la actividad de *Formar palabras* usando otras tarjetas que presenten en orden cada palabra formada; esto servirá para que los niños se den cuenta de ciertas estructuras del lenguaje. Por ejemplo, la maestra puede pedir a los niños que busquen todas las palabras que comienzan con /a/; todas las que terminan en /o/; todas las palabras que forman su plural añadiendo /s/ al final.

Para una descripción más detallada de estas actividades y otros ejemplos, vea Cunningham y Cunningham en *The Reading Teacher* de octubre de 1992.

Making Words

Cunningham and Cunningham (1992) describe an activity they call *Making Words* in which children segment the phonemes of orally presented words and move small letter cards to represent the words in print. This activity builds awareness and an understanding of letter-sound mapping. It is appropriate for children who know some letter-sound correspondences.

For this activity, each child is given a set of cards with selected letters written on them. The children are asked to use the letters to build words, beginning with two-letter words and progressing to words with more and more letters, until they use all the letters in the final word. For example, the children might be given the letter cards *a, o, g, l* and *s*. (The Cunninghams suggest that the children line up their cards with the vowels first and then the consonants in alphabetical order.) Then, the teacher asks them to select the two cards that spell the word *lo* (it). Children move the *l* and *o* into position to spell the word. Then, the teacher asks them to change one letter to spell the word *la* (the). Next, she tells them to add one letter to spell the word *las* (the). Children can be asked to spell the word *los* (the) and then to move the letters around to spell *sol* (sun), highlighting that the order of letters in words is important. From there, children are asked to spell *sola* (alone), *algo* (something), *lago* (lake), *lagos* (lakes) and *salgo* (I go out).

This activity draws attention to the sounds of word as children manipulate letter cards to spell the words. The *Making Words* activity can continue with the teacher using separate cards that display each of the words constructed in order to have children focus on certain patterns. For example, the teacher might want children to find all the words that begin with /a/, all the words that end with /o/, or the words that add /s/ at the end to make plurals.

For a detailed description of this activity and many examples, see Cunningham and Cunningham in the October 1992 issue of *The Reading Teacher*.

© Harcourt

Encuentren las letras que necesitamos para formar *lo*.

¿Qué letra tenemos que cambiar para formar *la*?

¿Qué letra necesitamos agregar para formar *las*?

¿Qué letra necesitamos cambiar para formar *los*?

Cambien el orden de las letras para formar *sol*.

¿Qué letra necesitamos agregar para formar *sola*?

Encuentren las letras que necesitamos para formar *algo*.

Cambien el orden de las letras para formar *lago*.

Añadan una letra para formar *lagos*.

¿Qué nueva palabra podemos formar con todas las letras que tenemos? (*salgo*)

CANCIONES PARA JUGAR CON SONIDOS

SONGS THAT PLAY WITH SOUNDS

A los niños pequeños les gusta cantar. Algunas canciones son muy útiles para ayudar a reconocer sonidos y a manipular el lenguaje. Las canciones que son aliterativas o que usan mucha rima requieren que se le preste atención a los sonidos. Las canciones en las que hay sustitución de fonemas o se añaden fonemas, ayudan a desarrollar la conciencia de que los sonidos en las palabras pueden ser manipulados. Las canciones con combinaciones de sonidos sin sentido exigen que los niños se fijen en el sonido en vez del significado. Incluidas aquí hay muchas canciones que ayudan a promover la conciencia fonémica. Estas canciones se pueden cantar tal como están escritas o la maestra puede animar a los niños a jugar con la lírica, añadiendo o cambiando versos o sustituyendo sonidos. Por ejemplo, en la canción "La mar estaba serena" los niños sustituyen las vocales cada vez que la repiten: La mar astaba sarana . . . ; Le mer estebe serene . . . ; Li mir istibi sirini . . . . Muchas canciones de niños que no están incluidas en este libro también se prestan para manipular los sonidos. Por ejemplo, en "Los pollitos dicen", los maestros pueden animar a los niños a sustituir la frase "pío, pío, pío" por "mío, mío, mío" o por "lío, lío, lío".

En las páginas siguientes hay una tabla que clasifica las canciones incluidas en este libro según el tipo de manipulación fonémica: rima, aliteración, sustitución de fonemas, manipulación de fonemas.

La música es un medio excelente para motivar a los niños a seguir aprendiendo, ya que las canciones se aprenden en el salón de clases, se practican en el patio de recreo y se comparten en la casa.

Young children enjoy singing. Some songs are especially useful for promoting an awareness of sounds and experimentation with and manipulation of language. Songs that are alliterative or make extensive use of rhyme demand attention to sounds. Songs in which there is phoneme substitution or addition help build an awareness that phonemes within words can be manipulated. Songs that make use of nonsensical combinations of sounds draw children's attention to the sound basis rather than the meaning basis of the lyrics. Included here are many songs that can be useful in promoting phonemic awareness. These songs may be sung as written or the teacher may encourage children to play with the lyrics by adding or changing verses or by substituting sounds. For instance, in the song "La mar estaba serena," children can substitute the vowels every time they sing: La mar estaba serena . . . ; Le mer estebe serene . . . ; Li mir istibi sirini. . . . Many well-known children's songs that are not included in this volume are appropriate for sound manipulation. For example, in the song "Los pollitos dicen," teachers can encourage children to substitute the phrase "pío, pío, pío," with "mío, mío, mío," or with "lío, lío, lío."

On the following pages is a chart listing each of the songs included in this volume, identified by type of phonemic manipulation; rhyme, alliteration, phoneme substitution, manipulation of phoneme.

Music is a wonderful medium for encouraging children to continue learning, as singing can "spill over" from the classroom onto the playground and into children's homes.

Guía para la planificación
Planning Guide

Fiesta fonémica: Canciones y actividades para desarrollar la conciencia fonémica y el casete *Fiesta fonémica* pueden ser utilizados para desarrollar la conciencia fonémica. Esta tabla detalla las canciones contenidas en este libro y la(s) destreza(s) que ayudan a desarrollar.

Canción Song	Sonido-letra *Sound-Letter*	Rima *Rhyme*	Aliteración *Alliteration*	Sustitución de fonemas *Phoneme Substitution*	Manipulación de fonemas *Nonsense Manipulation*
A ram sam sam	a			●	●
Mi sombrero de tres picos	b	●			
El juego del calentamiento	c		●		●
Chófer, chófer	ch	●			
Un dedo, un pulgar	d	●			
En la despensa	e	●			
En la feria	f	●		●	
Las gotitas de agua	g	●			
¿Has visto una muchacha?	h	●			
Anita me llamo, niña	i		●		
Gusanito medidor	j	●			
Canción de un círculo	l	●			
Caballito blanco	ll	●			
El chicle bola	m	●			
Cinco ratoncitos	n	●			

Canción / Song	Sonido-letra / Sound-Letter	Rima / Rhyme	Aliteración / Alliteration	Sustitución de fonemas / Phoneme Substitution	Manipulación de fonemas / Nonsense Manipulation
La muñequita	ñ	●			
Allá en la fuente	o	●			
Periquito	p		●		●
¡Qué linda manito!	q	●			
A la rueda, rueda	r	●			
¡Oh, Susana!	s	●			
Si tienes un gato	t	●			●
Sarasponda	u				●
Ruedas	v	●			
Me regalaron un violín	y	●		●	
Todo lo que como	z	●			
La mar estaba serena	vocales	●			

A ram sam sam

Moderato

A ram sam sam, a ram sam sam, Gu-li gu-li gu-li gu-li gu-li ram sam sam. A ra - fi, a ra - fi, Gu-li gu-li gu-li gu-li gu-li ram sam sam.

Mi sombrero de tres picos

Tres pi - cos mi som-bre - ro tres

pi - cos tie - ne sí. Si no tie -

ne tres pi - cos yo no lo quie - ro a -

sí.

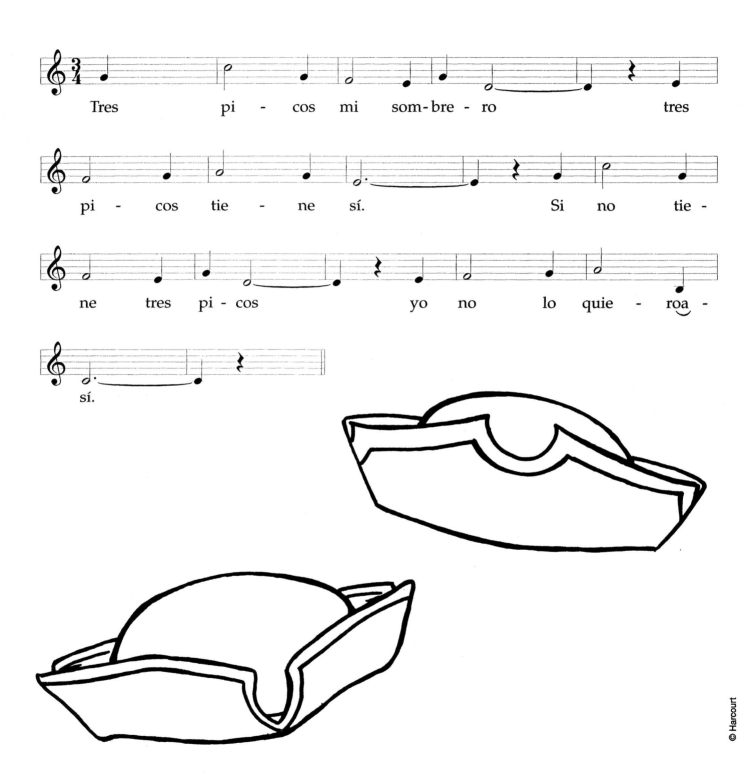

El juego del calentamiento

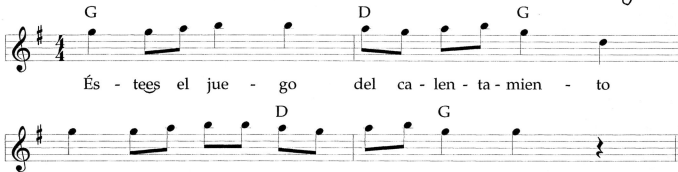

És - tees el jue - go   del ca - len - ta - mien - to

ha - brá que ver la ca - ra dees - car-mien - to

¡Jinetes, a la carga!
Una mano.

Éste es el juego del calentamiento
habrá que ver la cara de escarmiento
¡Jinetes, a la carga!
Una mano, la otra.

Éste es…
¡Jinetes, a la carga!
Una mano, la otra, el pie.

Éste es… ¡
Jinetes, a la carga!
Una mano, la otra, el pie, el otro.

Éste es…
¡Jinetes, a la carga!
Una mano, la otra, el pie, el otro,
   la cabeza.

Éste es…
¡Jinetes, a la carga!
Una mano, la otra, el pie, el otro,
   la cabeza, la cadera.

…la cadera, la otra, la rodilla, la otra,
   etc.

CHÓFER, CHÓFER

Moderato

Te - ne - mos un chó - fer que es

u - na ma - ra - vi - lla ma - ne - ja con los pies y

fre - na con las ro - di - llas chó - fer chó - fer

más ve - lo - ci - dad.

Un dedo, un pulgar

Moderato

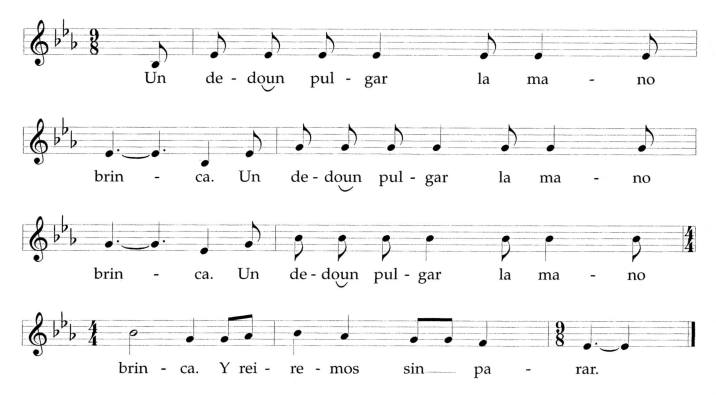

Un de - dou n pul - gar la ma - no brin - ca. Un de - dou n pul - gar la ma - no brin - ca. Un de - dou n pul - gar la ma - no brin - ca. Y rei - re - mos sin pa - rar.

2. Un dedo, un pulgar, la mano, la otra, brinca.
   Un dedo, un pulgar, la mano, la otra, brinca.
   Un dedo, un pulgar, la mano, la otra, brinca.
   Y reiremos sin parar.

Añadir:
3. Un brazo, etc.
4. El otro, etc.
5. Un pie, etc.
6. El otro, etc.
7. Arriba, abajo, etc.
8. Y gira, etc.

En la despensa

Judith Acoschky

En u - na des - pen - sa, un ra - tón en - tró,

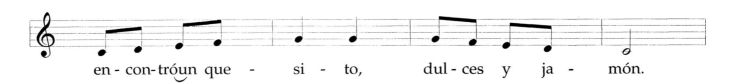

en - con - tró un que - si - to, dul - ces y ja - món.

Vino un gato negro
fijo lo miró
le pidió un poquito
y el ratón le dio.

En la feria

Allegro

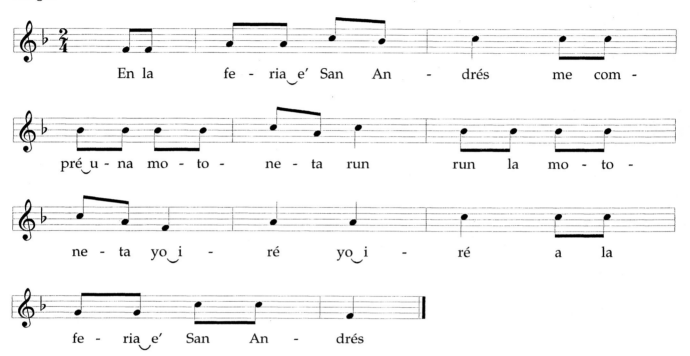

En la fe - ria e' San An - drés me com -
pré u - na mo - to - ne - ta run run la mo - to -
ne - ta yo i - ré yo i - ré a la
fe - ria e' San An - drés

En la feria e' San Andrés
me compré una bicicleta,
suis-suis... la bicicleta,
run-run... la motoneta.
Yo iré, yo iré,
a la feria e'San Andrés.

En la feria e' San Andrés
me compré una patineta,
crac-crac... la patineta,
suis-suis... la bicicleta,
run-run... la motoneta.
Yo iré, yo iré,
a la feria e' San Andrés.
(Y así, se siguen agregando palabras
    que terminen en "eta")

Las gotitas de agua

Que bo - ni - to jue - gan las go - ti - tas de agua,

las go - tit - as de agua de la re - ga - de - ra.

Sal - tan por los hom - bros jue - gan con el pe - lo y

por to - do el cuer - po van rue - da que rue - da.

Saltan a un tiempo
y me hacen gritar: !AH¡
Traviesas gotitas
que quieren jugar.

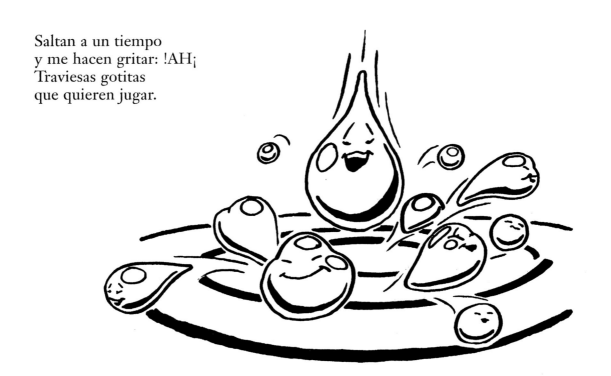

¿Has visto una muchacha?

Animato

Tradicional

¿Has vis - to una mu - cha - cha, mu - cha - cha, mu -

cha - cha? ¿Has vis - to una mu - cha - cha, bai - lar y sal -

tar? Y bai - la que bai - la y sal - ta que sal - ta. ¿Has

vis - to una mu - cha - cha bai - lar y sal - tar?

Anita me llamo, niña

Tradicional

Allegro

A - ni - ta me lla - mo, ni - ña, chin chin chi - ri - bi - ri - bín, chi - ri - bi - ri -

bán, soy hi - ja de un pes - ca - dor.

Cuando voy en mi barquita,
chin chin chiribiribín,
chiribiribán,
no le tengo miedo al calor.

Mi madre me dice: Niña,
chin chin chiribiribín,
chiribiribán,
hoy hace mucho calor.

Y yo le digo a mi madre
chin chin chiribiribín,
chiribiribán,
no le tengo miedo al calor.

Gusanito medidor

Gilda Rincón, Valentín Rincón y Omar Barros Rincón

Gu - sa - ni - to me - di - dor di - me cuán - to mi - do yo. Mí - de -
me des - de el za - pa - to, por la pier - na, por el bra - zo ¡Ay, ji - ji, ay, jo
jo! qué cos - qui - llas ten - go yo. ¡Ay, ji - ji, ay, jo jo! gu - sa -
ni - to me - di - dor.

Mido uno, mido dos,
mido veinte y un montón.

Cuatrocientos gusanitos
es la cuenta que ha salido.

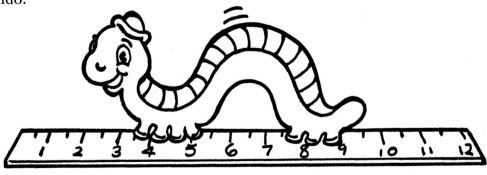

Canción de un círculo

Bryan A. Fitzgerald

Un cír - cu - lo tie - ne la for - ma del sol, La

for - ma de un dis - co, un pas - tel, un bo - tón. No tie - ne prin -

ci - pio tam - po - co fi - nal. Del cen - tro a la o - ri - lla

es siem - pre i - gual.

Caballito blanco

Tradicional

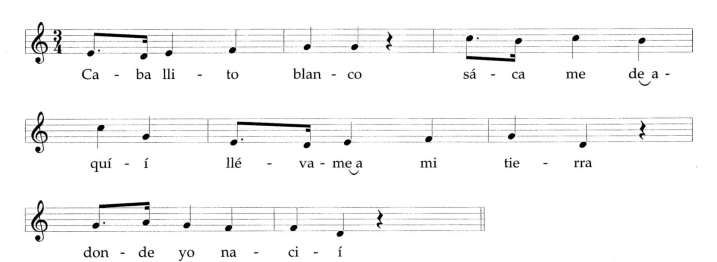

Ca - ba lli - to blan - co sá - ca me de a -

quí - í llé - va - me a mi tie - rra

don - de yo na - ci - í

Tengo, tengo, tengo…
Tú no tienes nada.
Tengo tres ovejas
en una cabaña:

Una me da leche,
otra me da lana,
otra mantequilla,
para la semana.

El chicle bola

Lois Lunt Metz

Vivo

Ma - má me dio mo - ne - das tan só - lo pa - ra mí, las

pu - se en mi bol - si - llo ya la tien - da yo co - rrí. A la má - qui - na de chi -

cles mi mo - ne - da yo le di y un chi - cle bo - la me dio a mí.

Chi - cle bo - la a mí me da, la má - qui - na de chi - cle es - pe - ran - do es - tá.

Cinco ratoncitos

Cin - co ra - ton - ci - tos   en - tran de la   cue - va

mue - ven el ho - ci - co   jue - gan a la   rue - da.

Cuatro ratoncitos
salen de la cueva
mueven el hocico
juegan a la rueda.

Tres ratoncitos…

Dos ratoncitos…

Un ratoncito
sale de la cueva
mueve el hocico
juega a la rueda.

Fiesta fonémica   **31**

La Muñequita

Andante   Tradicional

Ten - go u - na mu - ñe - ca ves - ti - da de a - zul,

con sus za - pa - ti - tos y su ca - mi - són.

Brinca la tablita,
yo ya la brinqué,
bríncala otra vuelta,
yo ya me cansé.

Dos y dos son cuatro,
cuatro y dos son seis,
seis y dos son ocho,
y ocho dieciséis,
y ocho veinticuarto,
y ocho treinta y dos.

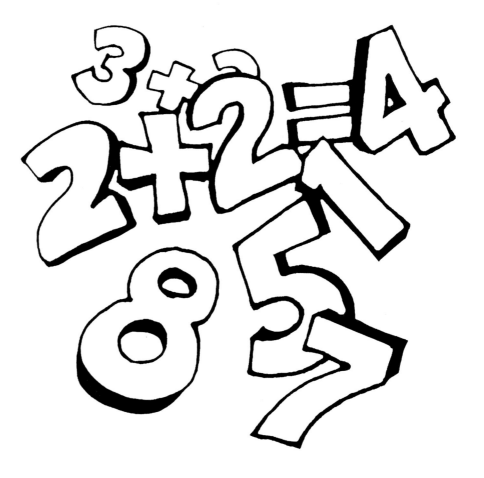

Allá en la fuente

A-llá en la fuen-te   ha-bía un cho-rri - to;   se ha-cía gran - do-te,   se ha-cía chi - qui-to;   es - ta - ba   de mal   hu - mor,   po - bre cho-rri - to   te-nía ca - lor.

Allá en la fuente,
las hormiguitas
están lavando
sus enagüitas,
porque el domingo
se van al campo
todas vestidas
de rosa y blanco.

Pero al chorrito
no le gustó
que lo vinieran
a molestar;
le dio vergüenza
y se escondió
tras de las piedras
de aquel lugar.

Periquito

Allegro

Pe - ri - qui - to Pe - ri - qui - to se - pa -

re - ce a su pa - pá por a - rri - ba - por de -

ba - jo por de - lan - te y por de - trás

¡Qué linda manito!

Qué lin - da ma - ni - to que tie - ne el be bé, qué

lin - da, qué mo - na, qué bo - ni - ta es.

Pequeños deditos rayitos de sol,
que gire que gire como un girasol.

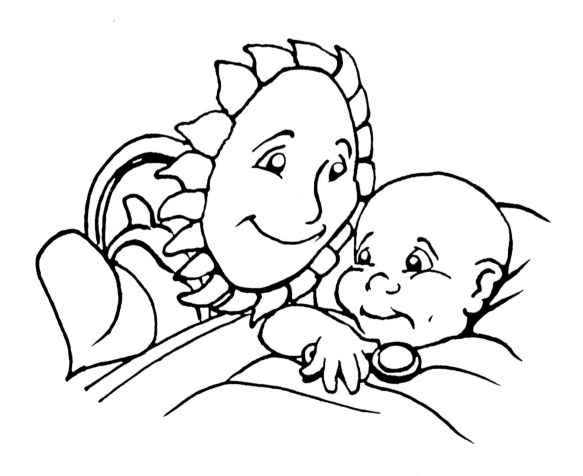

Fiesta fonémica   **35**

A la rueda, rueda

Allegro assai

Tradicional

A la rue - da, rue - da, de pan y ca - ne - la,

vís - te - le pron - to y ve pa - ra la es - cue - la.

Va - mos a can - tar, tam - bién a di - bu - jar.

¡Oh, Susana!

Allegro

A las seis de la ma - ña - na cuan - do

va a sa - lir el sol me le-van - to muy tem -

pra - no y sa - li - mos de ex - cur - sión.

¡Oh! Su - sa - na no llo - res más por

mí que me voy por la ma - ña - na y en la

tar de es - toy a quí.

En el monte de Arizona,
una chiva me encontré,
como no tenía nombre,
yo Susana la nombré.

¡Oh, Susana!
no llores más por mí,
que me voy por la mañana
y en la tarde estoy aquí.

Si tienes un gato

Dee Gibson

Si tienes dos gatos y dos te dan. Etc.
Si tienes tres gatos y uno te dan. Etc.
Si no tienes gatos y cuatro te dan. Etc.

Ruedas

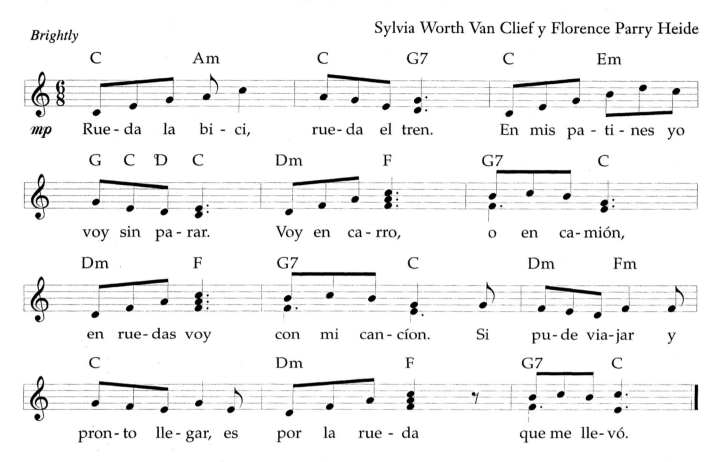

Sylvia Worth Van Clief y Florence Parry Heide

Brightly

| C | Am | C | G7 | C | Em |

mp Rue-da la bi - ci, rue-da el tren. En mis pa - ti - nes yo

| G | C | D | C | Dm | F | G7 | C |

voy sin pa - rar. Voy en ca - rro, o en ca - mión,

| Dm | F | G7 | C | Dm | Fm |

en rue-das voy con mi can - cíon. Si pu-de via-jar y

| C | Dm | F | G7 | C |

pron - to lle - gar, es por la rue - da que me lle - vó.

Fiesta fonémica

Sarasponda

voz primero

Bun - da bun - da   bun - da bun - da   bun - da bun - da   bun - da bun - da

voz segundo

Sa - ra - spon - da,   sa - ra - spon - da,   sa - ra - spon - da,   rut - sut - sut.

Bun - da bun - da   bun - da bun - da   bun - da bun - da   bun - da bun - da

Sa - ra - spon - da,   sa - ra - spon - da,   sa - ra - spon - da,   rut - sut - sut. A -

Me regalaron un violín

Para el día de mi santo me regalaron un violín.
Yi-ri-yin-yin, el violín, yi-ri-yi-yin, el violín.
Ay, qué dichosa yo me quedé; ay, qué dichosa yo me quedé.

Para el día de mi santo me regalaron un tambor.
Para-pon-pon, el tam bor, para-pon-pon, el tambor.
Ay, qué contenta yo me quedé;
ay, qué dichosa yo me quedé.

42   *Fiesta fonémica*

Todo lo que como

L. y M. Alberto Lozano

C   G7   C   F

To - do lo que co - mo lo co - mo pa - ra ser me - jor si lo a - pro-

C   G7   C   C   G7

ve - cho voy a ser muy fe - liz si to - do lo que co - mo lo co - mo pa - ra

C   F   C   G7   C   F

ser me - jor si lo a - pro - ve - cho voy a ser muy fe - liz dos ma - nos dos

C   G7   C   F

co - dos dos ro - di - llas y u - na na - riz pero hay que a - limentar la pi

C   G7   C   F   C   G7

pi - ta si quie - ro ser fe - liz pero hay que a - limentar la pi - pi - ta si quie - ro ser fe-

C

liz

Todo lo que como lo como para ser mejor; si lo aprovecho
voy a ser muy feliz; si todo lo que como lo como para ser
mejor; si lo aprovecho voy a ser muy feliz; dos tacos
dos mangos dos tortillas y una codorniz; porque
hay que alimentar la pipita si quiero ser feliz; porque
hay que alimentar la pipita si quiero ser feliz.

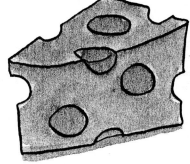

La mar estaba serena

Andante   Tradicional

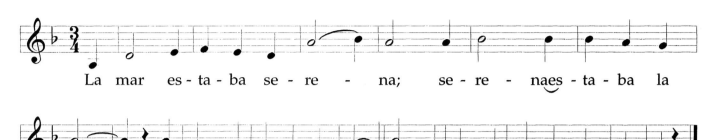

La mar es-ta-ba se - re - na; se - re - naes-ta-ba la

mar;_____ la mar es-ta-ba se - re - na, se-re-naes-ta-ba la mar._____

Libros para la lectura en voz alta que desarrollan la conciencia fonémica

Los libros para la lectura en voz alta son excelentes vehículos para desarrollar el conocimiento de la estructura de sonidos del lenguaje. A través de la repetición, combinación o sustitución de sonidos, o mediante el uso extenso de la rima, los libros ayudan a enfocar la atención en los sonidos. Aquí encontrará una lista de libros que son útiles para fijar la atención de los niños en los sonidos del lenguaje.

El rasgo más explícito y dominante en cada uno de estos libros es el uso que hacen del lenguaje, ya sea a través del juego de palabras o metáforas. Por lo tanto, los niños notarán que el lenguaje se usa para comunicar un mensaje. Además, los libros se prestan para jugar con el lenguaje aún más. La estructura de los libros es explícita y accesible, y sus contenidos lo suficientemente simples para que los niños puedan extender los cuentos.

Libros como éstos deben leerse una y otra vez. Los maestros deben motivar a los niños a notar el uso del lenguaje, a hacer predicciones y a decir cómo formaron sus predicciones. Por lo general, la respuesta tiene que ver con el uso que el autor hace del lenguaje. ("Ella está haciendo que las palabras rimen." "Él está comenzando todas las palabras con la misma letra.")

Read-Aloud Books that Develop Phonemic Awareness

Read-aloud books serve as excellent vehicles for developing many literacy insights, including the sound structure of language. Books that play with language by repeating sounds, mixing up sounds, substituting one sound for another, or making extensive use of rhyme help focus attention on sounds. Listed here are books that can be useful in helping children attend to the sounds of the language.

In each of these books, play with language is explicit and a critical, dominant feature. Thus, children are likely to notice the language that is used to communicate a message. And, the books lend themselves to further language play. Their patterns are explicit, their structures readily accessible, and the content simple enough that the stories can be extended by young children.

Books of this nature should be read over and over again. Teachers should encourage children to notice the language use, to have them make predictions, and tell how they derived their predictions. Generally, the answer will address the author's use of language. ("She's making the words rhyme." "He's starting every word with the same sound.")

NOTAS BIBLIOGRÁFICAS
ANNOTATED BIBLIOGRAPHY

Ada, Alma Flor. Días y días de poesía: Developing Literacy Through Poetry and Folklore. Hampton-Brown Books, 1991.

This book uses the instructional power of poetry by combining hundreds of authentic children's poems with over a hundred whole-language activities. Together, the poetry and activities help develop literacy and extend conceptual learning across the curriculum.

Bravo-Villasante, Carmen. El libro de los trabalenguas. Montena, 1991.

This assortment of tongue-twisting poems will have kids laughing at their own slip ups. The book offers over a hundred illustrated poems that help build children's language and reading skills.

Brown, Magaret Wise. Four Fur Feet. Doubleday, 1993.

In this simple book, the reader is drawn to the /f/ sound: the phrase "four fur feet" is repeated in every sentence as a furry animal walks around the world. We see four fur feet walk along the river, into the country, and so forth. The book must be turned around as the animal makes its way around the world.

Buller, Jon & Schade, Susan. I Love You, Good Night. Simon & Schuster, 1988.

A mother and child tell each other how much they love one another. When the child says "as much as blueberry pancakes," the mother responds that she loves her child as much as "milkshakes." The child says she loves her mother as much as "frogs love flies," to which the mother responds she loves her child as much as "pigs love pies." The two go back and forth in this manner until good night is said. The rhyme invites the listener to participate and continue the story.

Cameron, Polly. "I Can't." Said the Ant. Coward-McCann, 1961.

Household items discuss the fall of a teapot from the counter in a kitchen and the means by which to put it back. In a series of brief contributions to the conversation, each item says something that rhymes with its own name. "'Don't break her,' said the shaker" and "'I can't bear it,' said the carrot."

Carle, Eric. All About Arthur (An Absolutley Absurd Ape). Franklin Watts, 1974.

Arthur, an accordion-playing ape who lives in Atlanta, feels lonely and travels from Baltimore to Yonkers making friends. In each city he makes a friend whose name matches the initial sound of the city—from a banjo-playing bear in Baltimore to a young yak in Yonkers.

Carter, David A. More Bugs in Boxes. Simon & Schuster, 1990.

In this pop-up book, the reader is presented with a series of questions and answers about make-believe bugs that are found inside a variety of boxes. Both the questions and answers make use of alliteration: "What kind of bug is in the rosy red rectangle box? A bright blue big-mouth bug." Following a similar pattern is the author's Jingle Bugs (1992, Simon & Schuster) which has a Christmas theme and makes use of rhyme: "Who's in the chimney, warm and snug? Ho, ho, ho! It's Santa Bug!"

de Regniers, Beatrice Schenk, Moore, E., White, M. & Carr, J. Sing a Song of Popcorn. Scholastic, 1988.

A number of poems in this book draw attention to rhyme and can be used to encourage children to experiment with rhyme. Also included are poems that play with sounds within words. In "Galoshes," the author describes the slippery slush "as it slooshes and sloshes and splishes and sploshes" around a child's galoshes. In "Eletelephony," sounds are mixed up and substituted for one another— "Once there was an elephant, Who tried to use the telephant—"

Delacre, Lulu. Arroz con leche: Popular Songs and Rhymes from Latin America. Scholastic, 1989.

Full color illustrations accompany this collection of games, songs, and rhymes from Latin America. Text in English and Spanish allows any student to play and sing along with the musical scores available in the back of book.

Deming, A.G. Who Is Tapping at My Window? Viking Penguin, 1994.

A young girl hears a tap-tapping at her window and asks who is there. The farm animals each respond "It's not I" and she discovers that it is the rain. The book is predictable in that each pair of animals rhyme. The loon responds, followed by the raccon. The dog's response is followed by the frog's.

Díaz Roig, Mercedes & Miaja, María Teresa. Naranja dulce, limón partido: Antología de la lírica infantil mexicana. El Colegio de México, 1996.

This anthology of Mexican folk songs seeks to help preserve the tradition of Mexican children's music. It takes its songs, which are perfect for primary-grade students, from the archives of Seminario de Lírica Popular Mexicana del Centro de Estudios Lingüísticos y Literarios de El Colegio de México.

Ehlert, Lois. Eating the Alphabet: Fruits and Vegetables from A to Z. Harcourt Brace, 1989.

Fruits and vegetables are offered in print and pictures for each letter of the alphabet in this book. The following are displayed for B, for instance: blueberry, brussel sprouts, bean, beet, broccoli, banana.

Eichenberg, Fritz. Ape in a Cape. Harcourt Brace, 1980.

In this alphabet book of odd animals, we meet an ape in a cape, a pig in a wig, a rat with a bat, and others.

The original publication was named a Caldecott Honor Book.

Emberly, Barbara. One Wide River to Cross. Little, Brown, 1992.

This Caldecott Honor Book is a picture book adaptation of the traditional African-American spiritual about Noah's ark. Through the use of rhyme, the author describes the animals gathering on board one by one (while "Japhelth played the big bass drum"), two by two ("The alligator lost his shoe"), and so on up to ten, when the rains begin.

Fortunata. Catch a Little Fox. Scholastic, 1968.

In this repetitious book, children talk about going hunting. One by one they identify animals they will catch and where they will keep each one. A frog will be put in a log, a cat will be put in a hat, and so forth. The story concludes with the animals capturing the children, putting them in a ring and listening to them sing. Then they are released. The music is included in this book. A different version of this story that includes a brontosaurus (who is put in a chorus) and an armadillo (who is put in a pillow) is J. Langstaff's (1974) *Oh, A-Hunting We Will Go* published by Atheneum.

Galdone, Paul. Cat Goes Fiddle-i-fee. Clarion, 1985.

This is the old English rhyme that tells the story of a boy feeding his farm animals. As the animals are fed, they make noises: pig goes guffy guffy, the cat goes fiddle-i-fee, and the hen goes chimmy-chuck, chimmy-chuck. Sound repetition is a dominant part of this book.

Galdone, Paul. Henny Penny. Scholastic, 1968.

A hen becomes alarmed when an acorn hits her on the head. She believes the sky is falling, and on her way to inform the king she meets several animals who join her until they all get eaten by Foxy Loxy. This classic story is included here because of the amusing rhyming names of the animals. A more recent release of this story is Steven Kellogg's *Chicken Little* (1985) published by Mulberry Books, 1992.

Geraghty, Paul. Stop That Noise! Crown, 1992.

A mouse is annoyed with the many sounds of the forest and implores the the cicada to stop its "zee-zee-zee-zee," the frog to stop its "woopoo," until it hears far more disturbing sounds—the "Brrrm" and "Crrrrr RACKA-DACKA-RACKA-SHOONG" of a bulldozer felling trees. The presentation of animal and machine sounds make this book useful in drawing attention to the sounds in our language.

Gilman, P. The Wonderful Pigs of Jillian Jiggs. Scholastic, 1993.

"Jillian Jillian Jillian Jiggs, Maker of wonderful, marvelous pigs!" In this rhyming book, a young girl enthusiastically makes pigs to sell. When she realizes that she cannot part with them, she teaches others how to make them. Instructions for making pigs are included for the reader.

Gordon, Jeffie Ross. Six Sleepy Sheep. Puffin Books, 1991.

Six sheep try to fall asleep by slurping celery soup, telling spooky stories, singing songs, sipping simmered milk and so on. The use of the /s/ sound is prevalent throughout and amuses listeners as they anticipate the sheep's antics.

Hague, K. Alphabears. Henry Holt, 1984.

In this beautifully illustrated book, 26 teddy bears introduce the alphabet and make use of alliteration. Teddy bear John loves jam and jelly. Quimbly is a quilted bear and Pam likes popcorn and pink lemonade.

Hawkins, Colin & Jacqui. Tog the Dog. G.P. Putnam's Sons, 1986.

This book tells the story of Tog the Dog who likes to jog, gets lost in a fog, falls into a bog, and so forth. Emphasis is on words that rhyme with dog. With the exception of the final page, the pages in the book are not full width. On the final page the letters "og" appear in large bold type. As the reader turns the narrower pages throughout the text a new letter appears and lines up with the "og"—thus a new word

is presented on each page. When Tog falls into the bog, a large letter "b" lines up with the "og" to make the word, "bog." This is a great book for both developing phonemic awareness and pointing out a spelling pattern. Also by the authors are *Jen the Hen*, *Mig the Pig*, and *Pat the Cat*.

Hymes, Lucia & Hymes, James. Oodles of Noodles. Young Scott Books, 1964.

Several of the poems in this collection make use of nonsense words in order to complete a rhyme. In the poem "Oodles of Noodles," the speaker requests oodles of noodles because they are his/her favorite foodles. In a poem entitled "Spinach," the authors list a series of words each beginning with the /sp/ sound until they finally end with the word "spinach." Words include "spin," "span," "spun," and "spoony." Many of the other poems point out spelling patterns, and these will be entertaining to an older audience.

Krauss, Ruth. I Can Fly. Golden Press, 1958.

In this simple book, a child imitates the actions of a variety of animals. "A cow can moo. I can too." "I can squirm like a worm." "Howl howl howl I'm an old screech owl." The rhyming element combined with the charm of the child's imaginative play is what makes the story so engaging. On the final page, nonsense words that rhyme are used, encouraging listeners to experiment with sounds themselves: "Gubble, gubble gubble I'm a mubble in a pubble."

Kuskin, Karla. Roar and More. HarperTrophy, 1990

This book includes many poems and pictures that portray the sound that a variety of animals make. Both the use of rhyme and presentation of animal sounds ("Ssnnaaaarrll" for the tiger, "Hsssssss . . ." for the snake) draw children's attention to sounds. An earlier edition of this book won the 1979 NCTE Award for Excellence in Poetry for Children.

Let's Play Games in Spanish, Volume 2. National Textbook Company, 1986.

Looking to provide a break from the regular routines associated with foreign-language classrooms, this is the second of two volumes in a set that features games, skits, and songs as supplementary activities for Spanish-language classrooms.

Lewison, Wendy C. Buzz Said the Bee. Scholastic, 1992.

A series of animals sit on top of one another in this story. Before each animal climbs on top of the next it does something that rhymes with the animal it approaches. For instance, the hen dances a jig before sitting on the pig. The pig takes a bow before sitting on the cow.

Lindbergh, Reeve. The Day the Goose Got Loose. Viking Penguin, 1990.

Chaos results when a goose gets loose in this rhyming book. The horses were glad; they ran like mad. Mom was upset because the goose was a pet. The sheep were scared; they huddled and stared.

Martin, Bill, Jr. The Happy Hippopotami. Voyager Books, Harcourt Brace, 1991. Text copyright by Holt, Rinehart, and Winston, 1970.

This clever book makes use of rhyme and phoneme substitution as happy hippopotamamas wearing pretty beach pajamas and happy hippopotapoppas strolling about the candy shoppas have fun with family and friends at the beach.

Martin, Bill, Jr. Sounds of a Powwow. Holt, Rinehart, Winston, 1974.

Included in this volume is the song K-K-K-Katy in which the first consonant of several words is isolated and repeated, as in the song title. This song presents the opportunity for teachers to work with children on segmenting the sounds of their language.

Martin, Bill, Jr. and Archambault, John. Chicka Chicka Boom Boom. Scholastic, 1989.

The letters of the alphabet meet at the top of the coconut tree. Rhyme and silly play with sounds ("Skit skat skoodle doot. Flip flop flee.") make this book a must for preschool, kindergarten, and first grade teachers.

Martin, Bill, Jr. and Archambault, John. Listen to the Rain. Henry Holt, 1988.

This delightful book plays with language as the authors describe the rain, "Leaving all outdoors a muddle, a mishy, mushy, muddy puddle" and "The tiptoe pitter-patter, the splish and splash and splatter," making use of rhyme and medial sound substitution.

Martin, Bill, Jr. and Egielski, R. "Fire! Fire!" Said Mrs. McGuire. Harcourt Brace, 1971.

In this version of the well-known rhyme in which everyone's name rhymes with an exclamation for help, the fire is caused by the many candles on a birthday cake. The text is accompanied by colorful and often humorous illustrations.

Marzollo, J. The Teddy Bear Book. Dial, 1989.

Poems about teddy bears that the author adapted from songs, jump-rope rhymes, ball bouncing chants, cheers, and story poems are presented. Use of rhyme is considerable, from the well known, "Teddy bear, teddy bear, turn around, Teddy bear, teddy bear, touch the ground" to the less familiar, "Did you ever, ever, ever see a teddy bear dance with his wife" and the response, "No I never, never, never . . ." Play with sounds is obvious in the poem "Teddy Boo and Teddy Bear" where the author says, "Icabocker, icabocker, icabocker, boo! Icabocker, soda cracker, phooey on you!"

Marzollo, J. Ten Cats Have Hats. Scholastic, 1994.

A young child proudly shows a different hat on each page of this counting book as she tells the possessions of others: "Five ducks have trucks, but I have a hat," "Eight crabs have cabs, but I have a hat." The story is predictable, beginning with one bear and ending with ten cats, and makes obvious use of rhyme.

McDonald, Amy. Rachel Fister's Blister. Houghton Mifflin, 1990.

Rachel Fister gets a blister on her little toe. Her family enlists the aid of many people ("Find her brothers and some others . . ." "Call the palace. Ask Queen Alice . . .") and finally discovers that her mother's kiss makes the pain disappear.

Moerbeek, K. Can't Sleep. Price Stern Sloan, 1994.

In this highly repetitive pop-up book, a number of animals have difficulty sleeping because they think they are being watched. The /w/ sound is repeated more and more on each page as the fear mounts until the vulture shrieks, "Somebody is w-w-w-w-watching me!" The iteration of the /w/ and the elongation of the /s/ sound when a snake ssssighs focus attention on sounds in this story.

Most, Bernard. Cock-a-Doodle-Moo! Harcourt Brace, 1996.

A rooster discovers that it has lost its voice one morning and is unable to awaken everyone on the farm. Learning of the problem, a cow attempts to help but can't say "cock-a-doodle-doo" quite right. The resulting sound gives everyone an early morning laugh. This book makes use of phoneme addition and phoneme substitution and is a natural for developing a child's awareness of sounds.

El mundo de los niños, Poesías y canciones; Volumen 1. Salvat Editores, S.A., 1973.

This is the first book in a 15-volume set that serves as a guide to children's learning from pre-kindergarten until early adolescence. The first three books of the series specializes in introducing children to literature. Book one begins the introduction with a collection of traditional poems and songs that children can read themselves or parents can read aloud.

Obligado, Lilian. Faint Frogs Feeling Feverish and Other Terrifically Tantalizing Tongue Twisters. Viking Penguin, 1983.

For each letter of the alphabet, one or more tongue twisters using alliteration are presented in print and with humorous illustrations. "S" has smiling snakes sipping strawberry sodas, a shy spider spinning, and a swordfish sawing. "T" presents two toucans tying ties, turtles tasting tea, and tigers trying trousers.

Ochs, Carol. P. Moose on the Loose. Carolrhoda, 1991.

A moose escapes from the zoo in the town of Zown and at the same time a chartreuse caboose disappears. The zookeeper runs throughout the town asking citizens if they've seen a "moose on the loose in a chartreuse caboose." No one has seen the moose, but each has seen a different animal. Included among the many citizens is Ms. Cook who saw a pig wearing a wig, Mr. Wu who saw a weasel paint at an easel, and Mrs. Case who saw a skunk filling a trunk. Each joins in the search.

Orozco, José-Luis. De Colores and Other Latin American Folk Songs for Children. Dutton, 1994.

Twenty-seven songs, chants, and rhymes make up this anthology of Latin American folk music. Musical arrangements for piano, voice, and guitar accompany each set of English and Spanish lyrics. Suggestions for group sing-alongs, hand gestures, and games make this book perfect for classrooms and gatherings.

Otto, Carolyn B. Dinosaur Chase. HarperTrophy, 1991.

A mother dinosaur reads her young one a story about dinosaurs in which "dinosaur crawl, dinosaur creep, tiptoe dinosaur, dinosaur sneak." Both alliteration and rhyme are present in this simple, colorful book.

Parry, Caroline. Zoomerang-a-Boomerang: Poems to Make Your Belly Laugh. Puffin, 1991.

Nearly all of the works included in this collection of poems play with language, particularly through the use of predictable and humorous rhyme patterns. In "Oh my, no more pie," the meat's too red so the writer has some bread. When the bread is too brown, the writer goes to town, and so forth. In "What they said," each of twelve animals says something that rhymes with the type of animal it is. For instance, a pup says "Let's wake up," and a lark says "It's still dark." The pattern is similar to that presented in "I Can't," Said the Ant.

Patz, Nancy. Moses Supposes His Toeses Are Roses. Harcourt Brace, 1983.

Seven rhymes are presented here, each of which plays on language to engage the listener. Rhyme is predictable in "Sweetie Maguire" when she shouts "Fire! Fire!" and Mrs. O'Hair says, "Where? Where?" Alliteration makes "Betty Botter" a tongue twister: "But a bit of better butter—that will make my batter better!" Assonance adds humor to "The tooter" when a tooter tries to tutor two tooters to toot!

Pomerantz, Charlotte. If I Had a Paka. Mulberry, 1993.

A selection of twelve poems is included in this volume, and eleven languages are represented. The author manipulates words as in "You take the blueberry, I'll take the dewberry. You don't want the blueberry, OK Take the bayberry . . ." Many berries are mentioned, including a novel one—the "chuckleberry." Attention is drawn to phonemes when languages other than English are introduced. The Vietnamese translation of the following draws attention to rhyme and repetition: I like fish, Toy tik ka; I like chicken, Toy tik ga; I like duck, Toy tik veet; I like meat, Toy tik teet."

Prelutsky, Jack. The Baby Uggs Are Hatching. Mulberry, 1982.

Twelve poems describe unusual creatures such as the sneepies, the smasheroo, and the numpy-numpy-numpity. Though some of the vocabulary gets advanced (the Quossible has an irascible temper), most of the poems will be enjoyed by young children who will delight in the humorous use of words and sounds. For instance, "The Sneezysnoozer sneezes in a dozen sneezy sizes, it sneezes little breezes and it sneezes big suprises." In the poem that lends its name to the title of the book, children will hear sounds manipulated in nonsense words: "Uggily wuggily zuggily zee, and baby Uggs are fierce and free. Uggily wuggily zuggily zay, the baby Uggs come out today."

Prelutsky, Jack. Poems of A. Nonny Mouse. Knopf, 1989.

A. Nonny Mouse finally gets credit for all her works that were previously attributed to "Anonymous" in this humorous selection of poems that is appropriate for all ages. Of particular interest for developing phonemic awareness are poems such as "How much wood would a woodchuck chuck" and "Betty Botter bought some butter."

Provenson, Alice & Martin. Old Mother Hubbard. Random House, 1977.

In this traditional rhyme, Old Mother Hubbard runs errand after errand for her dog. When she comes back from buying him a wig, she finds him dancing a jig. When she returns from buying him shoes, she finds him reading the news. The rhyme element is a critical feature of this story.

Raffi. Down by the Bay. Crown, 1987.

In this story two young children try to outdo one another in making up rhymes with questions like, "Did you ever see a goose kissing a moose?" and "Did you ever see a bear combing his hair?" Music is included.

Raffi. Tingalayo. Crown, 1989.

Another of Raffi's songs is made into a book. Here the reader meets a man who calls for his donkey, Tingalayo, and describes its antics through the use of rhyme and rhythm. Phrases such as "Me donkey dance, me donkey sing, me donkey wearin' a diamond ring" will make children laugh.

Rosen, Michael, J. Poems for the Very Young. Kingfisher Books, 1993.

The author provides us with a selection of poems sure to engage young listeners. Many make use of rhyme ("Goodness gracious, fiddle dee dee, Somebody's grandmother out to sea"). Some make use of alliteration ("Lilly likes lollypops, lemonade and lime-drops"). Some make nonsensical play with sounds ("whipper-snapper, rooty-tooty, Helter-skelter, tutti-frutti").

Sendak, Maurice. Alligators All Around: An Alphabet. HarperTrophy, 1990.

Using alliteration for each letter of the alphabet, Sendak introduces the reader to the alphabet with the help of alligators who have headaches (for H) and keep kangaroos (for K).

Seuss, Dr. Dr. Seuss's ABC. Random House, 1963.

Each letter of the alphabet is presented along with an amusing sentence in which nearly all of the words begin with the targeted letter. "Many mumbling mice are making midnight music in the moonlight . . . mighty nice."

Seuss, Dr. Fox in Socks. Random House, 1965.

Before beginning this book the reader is warned to take the book slowly because the fox will try to get the reader's tongue in trouble. The play with language is the very obvious focus of this book. Assonance patterns occur throughout, and the listener is exposed to vowel sound changes when beetles battle, ducks like lakes, and ticks and clocks get mixed up with the chicks and tocks.

Seuss, Dr. There's a Wocket in My Pocket. Random House, 1965.

A child talks about creatures he has found around his house. These include a "nooth grush on my tooth brush" and a "zamp in the lamp." The initial sounds of common household objects are substituted with other sounds to make the nonsense creatures. A wonderful example of play with language!

Shaw, Nancy. Sheep on a Ship. Houghton Mifflin, 1989.

Sheep sailing on a ship run into trouble when facing a sudden storm. This entertaining story makes use of rhyme (waves lap and sails flap), alliteration (sheep on a ship), and assonance ("It rains and hails and shakes the sails"). Also by this author are *Sheep in a Jeep*, *Sheep out to Eat*, and *Sheep Take a Hike*.

Shelby, Anne. Potluck. Orchard, 1991.

Two friends, Alpha and Betty, organize a potluck and each of their friends contribute something. Christine came with carrot cake and corn on the cob. Monica made mounds and mounds of mashed potatoes. Alliteration draws attention to initial sounds throughout this book.

Showers, Paul. The Listening Walk. HarperTrophy, 1991.

A girl and her father go for a walk with their dog, and the listener is treated to the variety of sounds they hear while walking. These include "thhhhh . . . ," the steady whisper sound of some sprinklers and "whithh whithh," the sound of other sprinklers that turn around and around. Some phonemes are elongated as in "eeeeeeyowwwooo . . . ," the sound of a jet overhead. Some phonemes are substituted as in "bik bok bik bok," the sounds of high heels on the pavement.

Silverstein, Shel. Falling Up. HarperCollins, 1996.

Few children will not be entertained by the poetry of Shel Silverstein. In this latest collection there are many selections that play with sounds. For example, "My Nose Garden" begins, "I have rowses and rowses of noses and noses, And why they all growses I really can't guess." Sound substitiution, sound repetition and rhyme abound in these humorous and occasionally poignant poems.

Silverstein, Shel. A Giraffe and a Half. HarperCollins, 1964.

Using cumulative and rhyming patterns, Silverstein builds the story of a giraffe who has a rose on his nose, a bee on his knee, some glue on his shoe, and so on until he undoes the story by reversing the events.

Slepian, Jan. & Seider, A. The Hungry Thing. Scholastic, 1967.

One day a Hungry Thing shows up in town. Only a little boy can understand what the Hungry Thing would like to eat when the creature tells the townspeople he wants shmancakes. Shmancakes, says the little boy, "sound like Fancakes . . . sound like . . . Pancakes to me." Using sound substitution, the authors develop a clever tale in which the townspeople must play with sounds in common words ("boop with a smacker" is "soup with a cracker") in order to communicate with the Hungry Thing. Two other Hungry Thing books are: *The Hungry Thing Returns* and *The Hungry Thing Goes to a Restaurant*.

Staines, Bill. All God's Critters Got a Place in the Choir. Viking Penguin, 1989.

This lively book makes use of rhyme to tell of the place that numerous animals—an ox and a fox, a grizzly bear, a possum and a porcupine, bullfrogs—have in the world's choir. "Some sing low, some sing higher, some sing out loud on the telephone wire."

Tallon, Robert. Zoophabets. Scholastic, 1979.

Letter by letter, the author names a fictional animal and in list form tells where it lives and what it eats. All, of course, begin with the targeted letter. "Runk" lives in "Rain barrels" and eats "raindrops, rusty rainbows, ripped rubbers, raincoats, rhubarb."

Urdaneta, Josefina. Si canto... Latinoamerica, C.A., 1995.

This book brings together into one collection traditional poems, such as "Pepito Zanahoria" and "París se quema," with newer ones, like "Soy" and "La cuchilla." This compilation is a fun way to initiate students into an understanding of language and poetry.

Van Allsburg, Chris. The Z was Zapped. Houghton Mifflin, 1987.

A series of mishaps befalls the letters of the alphabet. "A" is crushed by an avalanche, "B" is bitten badly, "C" is cut to ribbons, and so forth. Other alphabet books using alliteration include G. Base's *Animalia* (1987) published by Harry N. Abrams, K. Greenaway's *A Apple Pie* (1993) published by Derrydale, and J. Patience's *An Amazing Alphabet* (1993) published by Random House.

West, Colin. "I Don't Care!" Said the Bear. Candlewick, 1996.

A cocky bear (with his nose in the air) is not afraid of a loose moose, a big pig, a snake from a lake, or other such animals, but he runs from the teeny weeny mouse. Ryhme is used throughout this book.

Winthrop, E. Shoes. HarperTrophy, 1986.

This rhyming book surveys many familiar and some not-so-familiar types of shoes. The book begins, "There are shoes to buckle, shoes to tie, shoes too low, and shoes too high." Later we discover, "Shoes for fishing, shoes for wishing, rubber shoes for muddy squishing." This rhythm and rhyme book invites participation and creative contributions.

Wood, Audrey. Silly Sally. Harcourt Brace, 1992.

Rhyme and alliteration are obvious in this book about Silly Sally who goes to town and makes some acquaintances along the way. She does a jig with a pig, plays leapfrog with a dog, and sings a tune with a loon.

Zemach, Margot. Hush, Little Baby. E. P. Dutton, 1976.

In this lullaby, parents attempt to console a crying baby by promising a number of outrageous things including a mockingbird, a diamond ring, a billy goat, and a cart and bull. The verse is set to rhyme, e.g., "If that cart and bull turn over, Poppa's gonna buy you a dog named Rover," and children can easily innovate on the rhyme and contribute to the list of items being promised.

BIBLIOGRAFÍA
BIBLIOGRAPHY

Adams, M.J. (1990). Beginning to Read: Thinking and Learning About Print. Cambridge, MA: MIT Press.

Arnold, A. (1964). The Big Book of Tongue Twisters and Double Talk. New York: Random House.

Ball, E. & Blachman, B. (1988). Phoneme segmentation training: Effect on reading readiness. Annals of Dyslexia, 38, 208–225.

Blachman, B. (1991). Getting Ready to Read: Learning How Print Maps to Speech. Washington, D.C.: U.S. Department of Health and Human Services.

Bradley, L. & Bryant, P. (1983). Categorizing sounds and learning to read—a causal connection. Nature, 301, 419–421.

Clark, H.H. & Clark, E.V. (1977). Psychology and Language. New York: Harcourt Brace Jovanovich.

Cole, J. (1989). Anna Banana. New York: Beechtree Paperback.

Cunningham, A.E. (1990). Explicit versus implicit instruction in phonemic awareness. Journal of Experimental Child Psychology, 50, 429–444.

Cunningham, P., & Cunningham, J. (1992). Making words: enhancing the invented spelling-decoding connection. The Reading Teacher, 46(2), 106–115.

Emrich, D. (1970). The Nonsense Book. New York: Four Winds Press.

Ehri, L. (1984). The development of spelling knowledge and its role in reading acquisition and reading disability. Journal of Learning Disabilities, 22, 356–365.

Geller, L.G. (1983). Children's rhymes and literacy learning: Making connections. Language Arts, 60, 184–193.

Geller, L.G. (1982a). Grasp of meaning: Theory into practice. Language Arts, 59, 571–579.

Geller, L.G. (1982b). Linguistic consciousness-raising: Child's play. Language Arts, 59, 120–125.

Griffith, P.L. & Olson, M.W. (1992). Phonemic awareness helps beginning readers break the code. The Reading Teacher, 45(7), 516–523.

Loredo, E. (1996). The Jump Rope Book. New York: Workman.

Lundberg, I., Frost, J. & Peterson, O. (1988). Effects of an extensive program for stimulating phonological awareness in preschool children. Reading Research Quarterly, 23, 263–284.

Mattingly, I. (1984). Reading, linguistic awareness, and language acquisition. In J. Downing & R. Caltin (Eds.), Language Awareness and Learning to Read (pp. 9–25). New York: Springer Verlag.

Stanovich, K.E. (1986). Matthew effects in reading: Some consequences of individual differences in the acquisition of literacy. Reading Research Quarterly, 21, 360–407.

Stanovich, K.E. (1994). Romance and reality. The Reading Teacher, 47(4), 280–291.

Yopp, H.K. (1988). The validity and reliability of phonemic awareness tests. Reading Research Quarterly, 23, 159–177.

Yopp, H.K. (1992) Developing phonemic awareness in young children. The Reading Teacher, 45(9), 696–703.

Yopp, H.K. (1995a). Read-aloud books for developing phonemic awareness: An annotated bibliography. The Reading Teacher, 48, 538–542.

Yopp, H.K. (1995b). A test for assessing phonemic awareness in young children. The Reading Teacher, 49(1), 20–29.